Ferret

Curious Kids Press

The Ferret

The Ferret is not a rodent. It belongs to the family of Mustelidae. Weasels and polecats are also in this family. Ferrets are the third most popular pet in the U.S. A male Ferret is called a Hob, a female is a Jil and a baby Ferret is a Kit. Let's discover more fun things about the Ferret and explore its world. We will uncover facts about the wild Ferret and the tame Ferret. Read on..

Where in the World?

Did you know the Ferret originated in Europe? These animals were used to hunt rabbits. Today Ferrets can be found as pets all over the world. However, some places will not allow you to bring Ferrets into the country. New Zealand once had a problem with wild Ferrets eating their native birds.

The Body of a Ferret

Did you know the Ferret is long and slender? The body of an adult Ferret can measure up to 20 inches long (51 centimeters). The tail of the Ferret is another 5 inches in length (13 centimeters). The Ferret has short legs and a pointy snout. Its ears are small and stand straight up.

The Ferret's Fur

Did you know the Ferret has short soft fur? Their fur can be brown, black, white or a mix of colors. The Ferret also has a musky scent on its body. In the wild, the Ferret uses its scent glands to mark its territory. The scent glands are sometimes removed on pet Ferrets.

The Ferrets Teeth

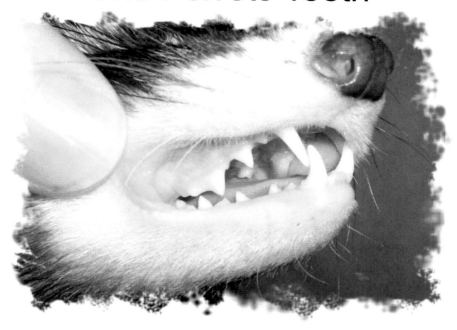

Did you know the Ferret has very sharp teeth? They have 4 big canine teeth at the front of their mouth These are used in the wild for hunting prey. The smaller teeth help this animal chew up its food. When Ferrets play, they will nip playfully. This can hurt, so be careful when you play with this animal.

What the Ferret Eats

Did you know in the wild Ferrets eat meat? This includes the meat, organs, bones, skin fur or feathers of animals and birds. However, pet Ferrets should be fed a high-grade dry cat food. There is also Ferret food made specially for them. This can be found in pet stores. Ferrets also need to have fresh water available at all times.

The Ferret's Special Ability

Did you know the Ferret will do a weasel war dance? This joyful and fun-to-watch dance is done when the Ferret is very excited or happy. It will bounce sideways, hopping and bumping into things. It may look silly, but this means the Ferret is having a lot of fun.

Ferrets at Rest

Did you know Ferrets are more active at night? This is called being, nocturnal. Ferrets will start to move about at dusk and stay busy until dawn. If the Ferret is out in the wild, it would do most of its hunting at night. Pet Ferrets like to play with toys and chase each other around.

Ferrets as Predator

Did you know Ferrets will prey on most anything? In the wild, Ferrets will prey on birds, small rodents and even eggs. The favorite prey of a Ferret are wild rabbits. The Ferret will go down into the rabbit's underground burrow. If the rabbit tries to flee the Ferret will grab it with its sharp teeth.

The Ferrets as Prey

Did you know the Ferret has natural enemies? In the wild, Ferrets are hunted by large birds of prey, such as hawks and eagles. Larger animals will also hunt the Ferret. Sometimes it isn't an animal or bird that takes a Ferret, it is disease. Also, the loss of habitat will also harm wild Ferrets.

Ferrets as Pets

Did you know Ferrets make fun pets? If you want a Ferret for a pet, you will have to keep it in a special cage. It will need bedding, a food dish and a water bottle. The Ferret will want to play, so you should give it plenty of toys and exercise. Ferrets also need to be bathed, just like a dog does.

Ferret Talk

Did you know Ferrets can make sounds? The Ferret can make some strange noises. It will make a soft "clucking" sound This is called, "dooking" and is usually done when the Ferret is happy or playful. If a Ferret gets frightened it will hiss. If a Ferret is upset or worried it will make a soft squeaking noise.

Mom Ferret

Did you know the female Ferret can have 1 to 15 babies in one litter? The mother Ferret will nurse her babies milk from her body. She will have her babies in a den or shelter where they are safe. In her den she will make a nest for her babies.

Baby Ferrets

Did you know baby Ferrets are born pink? They are also born blind. After about 34 days the kits will open their eyes. By this age they will also be growing their fur in.   When Ferrets are around 10 weeks-of-age, they will begin to show their personalities. This can be a fun time for a Ferret owner.

Life of a Ferret

Did you know the Ferret spends most of its life sleeping? The Ferret will spend from 18 to 20 hours a day sleeping. When its not sleeping it will be playing and eating. A healthy Ferret can live to be from 7 to 10 years old. A tame Ferret should be taken to the vet and have vaccinations, just like a dog or a cat.

Quiz

Question 1: How long does an adult Ferret measure?

Answer 1: 20 inches (51 centimeters)

Question 2: What does the Ferret have on its fur?

Answer 2: A musky scent

Question 3: What special ability does the Ferret have?

Answer 3: It will do the weasel war dance

Question 4: What does a tame Ferret eat?

Answer 4: High-grade cat food or ferret food

Question 5: When is the Ferret most active?

Answer 5: Dusk to dawn

Thank you for checking out another title from Curious Kids Press! Make sure to search "Curious Kids Press" on Amazon.com for many other great books.

Made in the USA
Middletown, DE
18 April 2022

64447685R00018